MW01286626

AFRICAN AMERICAN HISTORY MONTH
Daily Devotions 2005

Karen F. Williams

Abingdon Press
Nashville

African American History Month
Daily Devotions 2005

0-687-341841

Copyright © 2005 by Karen F. Williams

This book is printed on acid-free paper.

All scripture quotations unless noted otherwise are taken from the *New Revised Standard Version of the Bible,* copyright 1989 by the Division of Christian Education of the National Council of the Churches of Christ in the United States of America. Used by permission. All rights reserved.

Scripture quotations noted NIV are taken from the HOLY BIBLE, NEW INTERNATIONAL VERSION. Copyright © 1973, 1978, 1984 by International Bible Society. Used by permission of Zondervan Publishing House. All rights reserved.

Scripture quotations marked CEV are from the *Contemporary English Version,* © 1991, 1992, 1995 by American Bible Society. Used by permission.

Scripture quotations marked GNT are from the Good News Translation in Today's English Version—Second Edition © 1992 by American Bible Society. Used by Permission.

Scripture quotations marked Message are from *THE MESSAGE.* Copyright © Eugene H. Peterson, 1993, 1994, 1995. Used by permission of NavPress Publishing Group.

Scripture quotations marked NKJV are taken from the New King James Version. Copyright © 1982 by Thomas Nelson, Inc. Used by permission. All rights reserved.

Scripture quotations marked NLT are from the *Holy Bible,* New Living Translation, copyright © 1996. Used by permission of Tyndale House Publishers, Inc., Wheaton, Illinois 60189. All rights reserved.

Introduction

We must give our own story to the world.
—Carter G. Woodson

Stories are powerful. They can change the way we think and act. They can affect a life, a family, a community, a generation. Dr. Carter G. Woodson, the Father of Black History, is one storyteller who developed the structure for African American history. His expositions on education, African culture, the African American church, the wage earner, and history in general marked the beginning of instructing the world of an overlooked and a misinterpreted history. He wanted to inform, so he told the African American story in as many ways as possible. Through books, articles, journals, organizations, and the academic system he told the story.

This edition of *African American History Month Daily Devotions* continues to tell the story. In this collection you will hear familiar stories and some unfamiliar ones. These are radical stories of people who dared to be different, to be courageous, to take a stand. Their visions, inventions, actions changed the world. Jesus, our Redeemer, is the initiator of radical stories, for his birth, life, death, and resurrection are revolutionary. He too told radical stories, in the form of parables and similes. Thus these meditations interweave Jesus' parables with stories of heritage. These daily devotions also highlight Dr. Woodson's legacy by providing facts about his life as well as quotations by him.

My hope is that as you encounter these stories of faith and heritage you will not only be enlightened but also transformed by the power of the gospel.

—Karen F. Williams

Documentation does not exist to confirm the exact date of birth for some persons mentioned in this devotional. In such cases I have used either (?) or "circa."

TUESDAY, FEBRUARY 1, 2005

PROPHETS IN THE VALLEY

*I prophesied as the [Lord God] commanded me,
and the breath came into them, and they lived,
and stood on their feet, a vast multitude.*
(Ezekiel 37:10)

Read Ezekiel 37:1-14

The land slopes and is narrow and dry. It is a valley full of dry bones. Right in the middle of the valley is the prophet Ezekiel. The bones Ezekiel sees are scattered all over. "Can these bones live?" God asks. Ezekiel's response displays his trust in God's omniscience: "O Sovereign Lord, you alone know" (Ezekiel 37:3*b*). But these are no ordinary bones. They are bones of assurance, for God promised restoration and deliverance to Israel, to gather them and bring them to their own land (Ezekiel 36:24). So right there in the midst of death and hopelessness, God commands Ezekiel to prophesy, to speak the word to bones. When Ezekiel speaks, the transformation begins. The bones come together. Flesh appears. Breath enters. Life comes. The bones stand. They become an army—a vast army.

American slavery was a valley for African Americans. Yet in the midst of this valley of hopelessness, God had many prophetic voices who spoke of deliverance. These were the abolitionist voices of William Still (1821–1902), Sojourner Truth (1797–1883), James Forten (1766–1842), David Walker (circa 1785–1830), and a long history of orators. These pioneers spoke in the valley and brought hope. Slavery, as dehumanizing and cruel as it was, did not bring the African American race to extinction. With God's help and abolitionist voices throughout our history, we survived. We have breath, we live, and we stand like a vast army.

May we be ever mindful to speak, as God commands, words of hope in our valleys. Let's speak life, hope, deliverance, and victory.

Prayer: Lord, help me to speak as you command, and bring life and hope to others.

Dr. Carter G. Woodson was born 1875 in New Canton, Virginia.

WEDNESDAY, FEBRUARY 2, 2005

THE HEART OF THE MATTER

*Create in me a clean heart, O God,
and put a new and right spirit within me.*
(Psalm 51:10)

Read 2 Samuel 12:1-11

What would make a rich man with a large herd of sheep and cattle steal a poor man's only sheep? This action is the epitome of greed and evil. David thought so and was outraged when Nathan told the story of the poor man's stolen sheep. But his outrage soon turned to repentance when Nathan revealed that David was the rich man in the story. David's sinful actions—adultery with Bathsheba, marriage to her, and murder of Uriah—displeased God and revealed the selfishness and evil status in David's heart.

One woman's action is an antithesis to that of the unscrupulous rich man in this story. This woman was born in Hattiesburg, Mississippi, in 1908. She once described herself as "just a little old colored woman who walked everywhere." She, like the poor man in Nathan's parable, had little. She had little education, a little job—she washed and ironed clothes for seventy-five years. Her job yielded little income, but she saved as much as she could. She did not save for herself but for others. And in 1995 she established a $150,000 trust fund for students attending the University of Southern Mississippi in Hattiesburg. This little woman with a big heart of love was Oseola McCarty.

Both McCarty (who died in 1999) and the rich man in Nathan's parable can teach us much about the nature of our hearts. Are we stealing from others because of our greed? Perhaps it is not the physical act, but we can steal by keeping what we could give away to others. Are we giving to others? We can give not just money but our time and talents with a heart of love.

Prayer: Loving God, create in me a clean heart.

Woodson received a bachelor of literature degree from Berea College (1903).

Oseola McCarty's *Simple Wisdom for Rich Living* (Marietta, Ga.: Longstreet Press, 1996).

THE FOOLPROOF PLAN

*And I'll say to myself, "You have plenty of good things
laid up for many years. Take life easy, eat, drink, and be merry."*
(Luke 12:19, NIV)

Read Luke 12:13-21

The rich man had a foolproof plan. His infallible plan was to build a barn large enough to store all his fruit and goods. These goods would last for years. He had riches, plenty of food, and plans for a good time. In his mind he had it all.

The rich man did not have it all. He factored out God. His foolproof plan only proved that he was the fool. God says to him, "Tonight you will die. Then who will get what you have stored up" (Luke 12:20, CEV).

Are we easily deceived, like the rich man, by placing too much emphasis on material possessions rather than on God? Although jobs, money, and clothes are the necessities of life, God does not want us to let these things absorb us so that we think only of ourselves. The rich man could have shared his wealth with the less fortunate. But he kept it all for himself.

No matter what we obtain in this life, we must remember that our dependence must be on God. Dr. Martin Luther King, Jr., expounds on this parable by saying that the self-absorbed rich man thought he was God: "[The rich man] talked as though he unfolded the seasons . . . controlled the rising and the setting of the sun, and regulated the natural processes that produce the rain and the dew."

In reality the rich man was poor because he placed his dependence on temporal riches, and he was not rich toward God.

We are rich toward God when we treasure living a righteous and obedient life for Christ. By doing so, we store up a treasure, a solid foundation for our future (1 Timothy 6:19).

Prayer. Lord, I appreciate all the material blessings you provide for me, but my desire is to be rich toward you through righteous living.

Woodson taught in the Philippines (1903–1907).

Martin Luther King, Jr., *Strength to Love* (Cleveland: Collins & World, 1977).

THE FOOLPROOF PLAN CONTINUED

*Abraham said, "Child, remember that during your lifetime
you received your good things, and Lazarus in like manner evil
things; but now he is comforted here, and you are in agony."*
(Luke 16:25)

Read Luke 16:19-32

The O'Jays hit song "For the Love of Money," recorded more than thirty years ago, details what people will do for money. People will lie, cheat, steal, among other immoral things. The lyrics later warn "don't let money fool you." That's what happened in this parable. Another wealthy man fooled by riches.

Unlike the previous story, this parable goes further by telling what happens to the rich man. He finds himself in hell, full of agony. While the poor man, Lazarus, goes to heaven. What a contrast. But the nature of their lives was a disparity.

The response Abraham gives the rich man when he requests mercy sums it well: "During your lifetime you received your good things." This shows us that the rich man was not preparing himself for heaven, eternal life. He made his possessions heaven. They brought him comfort. However, the poor man invested in heavenly treasures, and so now in the end is comforted.

We too must not let money fool us, but should invest in heavenly treasures by first seeking God (Luke 12:3) and realizing that all we have belongs to him.

Prayer: Dear Lord, money is not everything, but you are. Thank you for being the All-Sufficient One.

**Woodson received B.A. and M.A. degrees from the
University of Chicago (1908).**

THE POTTER'S MESSAGE

Go down to the potter's house, and there I will give you my message.
(Jeremiah 18:2, NIV)

Read Jeremiah 18:1-10

The potter's house served as a pulpit and was the place where God delivered a message to Jeremiah. When the pot he was making became marred, the potter did not despair. Despite the defect, he continued making his masterpiece by shaping it into another pot. God likened Israel to the marred pot. If Israel remained in the Potter's hands, moldable like the clay, God promised to shape it into something new and marvelous: "O house of Israel, can I not do with you as the potter does?" (v. 5).

William Edmondson (circa 1882–1951), a Tennessee sculptor, was a fine example of one who remained in the potter's hands. God used Edmondson's own hands in a remarkable way. He was the first African American artist to have a one-man exhibition at New York's Museum of Modern Art. Edmondson, noted for his tombstones and limestone figures, said God told him to make sculptures: "I was out in the driveway with some old pieces of stone when I heard a voice telling me to pick up my tools and start to work on a tombstone. . . . God was telling me to cut figures. First He told me to make tombstones; then He told me to cut the figures."

We are in the Potter's hands. God makes of us what he will. But we have to be pliable, open to God's call. We, like Jeremiah and Edmondson, have to be attentive, and God will give us a message too. And all that God allows us to craft will speak words of hope and promise. We just have to remain in his hands. God's dexterity is sufficient.

Prayer: O Capable Potter, please mold me and shape me according to your will.

Woodson received a Ph.D. in history from Harvard University in 1912, the second African American to receive this degree. W.E.B. DuBois was the first.

Edmund L. Fuller, *Visions in Stone: The Sculpture of William Edmondson* (London: Media Directions, 1973).

SUNDAY, FEBRUARY 6, 2005

BUILDING ON UNDERSTANDING

*When the storm has swept by, the wicked
are gone, but the righteous stand firm forever.*
(Proverbs 10:25, NIV)

Read Matthew 7:24-27

Jesus knows a discrepancy exists between what we do and what we say. Thus he precedes the parable of the two builders with a warning in Matthew 7:21-23. This caution is to those who are always calling the Lord's name but are not doing what he says. There is also an incongruity between hearing and doing, which Jesus presents in the parable of the two builders. The builder who uses sand as a foundation deceives himself by thinking his house is stable. This builder is oblivious to the fact a storm would come someday. Or perhaps he takes the shortcut intentionally, thinking he will establish a firm foundation later. Yet the example that Jesus applauds is the person who builds the foundation on a rock. Jesus says this person hears the word and obeys it. In doing so, this builder constructs a solid foundation, a foundation that no storm can destroy.

A foundation is essential. It is groundwork from which everything is built. Carter G. Woodson, named the Father of Black History, laid a historical foundation. Woodson published numerous books and articles, which have been a primary source of research for scholars.

Much has taken place since Woodson's initial works, but his works have stood the test of time and the storms of life. He didn't merely hear about the need for black history to be recognized, but he put his thoughts and words into action. Our faith too will withstand the storms of life, if built on the foundation of Jesus, our Rock.

Prayer: God, my Solid Rock, I have made you my foundation.

**Woodson: "Not to know what one's race has done in former times
is to continue always a child."** *(The Story of the Negro Retold, 1935)*

WISDOM WINS

Wisdom is better than strength.
(Ecclesiastes 9:16*a*, NIV)

Read Ecclesiastes 9:13-18

The little city and its few inhabitants were in trouble. A king threatened to attack it. What could the people do to protect themselves against a powerful king? They had no army, inadequate weapons, and little authority in comparison to the king. They were defenseless, at least the king thought so. Yet they were armed with one unsuspected weapon. This weapon was a poor man—a poor man with wisdom. This poor man was enough, and he used his wisdom to save the city.

The Scriptures do not tell us specifically what this man did to save his city, but his wisdom commandeered a powerful king and rendered his siege a failure. Through this parable Solomon concludes that wisdom is better than strength. Wisdom can subdue wars.

Wisdom fights battles for us by providing insight, direction, protection, which lead to a changed life. The Bible contains more than 200 references to wisdom, many of them located in Proverbs. We also can gain insights from African proverbs. One Nigerian proverb states, *However far the stream flows, it never forgets its source.* A West African proverb states, *Silence is also a form of speech.* A Moroccan saying goes, *Little and lasting is better than much and passing.*

Let's learn to seek and accept wisdom. It can render our enemy powerless.

Prayer: Lord, grant me wisdom.

Woodson: *After Negro students have mastered the fundamentals of English . . . they should direct their attention also to the folklore of the African, to the philosophy in his proverbs.*
(*The Mis-Education of The Negro*)

NEW WINE, NEW LIFE

New wine must be put into new wineskins.
(Mark 2:22c, CEV)

Read Mark 2:21-22

Why does Jesus eat with tax collectors and sinners? How can Jesus tell someone "Your sins are forgiven?"
Jesus was disturbing the status quo, and the Pharisees wanted to know why. Jesus addresses these questions in Mark 2, illuminating his answer with parables. The parables state that you cannot mix the new with the old. A new patch is useless on an old garment, for the new cloth will shrink and cause a worst tear. Likewise new wine is wasted when placed in old jugs, for unfermented wine will burst the aged jars. This happens because new wine, while fermenting, causes the jars to swell. Since old jars were stiff and without elasticity, they would burst.

The Pharisees were rigid like the old wineskins. Their pseudo piety did not extend itself to Jesus' "radical" theology. But Jesus wanted to widen the spiritual horizons of this religious group, and to let them know that he, the Son of God, brings a whole new way of living. Yet the new is often met with opposition.

Jackie Robinson (1919–1972) experienced this opposition on the baseball field. As the first African American to play with a major baseball league, the Brooklyn Dodgers, he was confronted with acts of racial hatred. He broke the color line.

Jesus also shattered a line: the religious line. He introduced the world to a new way of thinking. Jesus is the new wine. And if we accept the salvation that he offers, we too will have a new way of life.

Prayer: Jesus, help me to embrace the new life you offer.

**Woodson established the Association for the
Study of Negro Life and History (1915).**

THE SOIL OF UNDERSTANDING

*And the seeds sown in the good soil stand for those
who hear the message and understand it: they bear fruit.*
(Matthew 13:23, GNT)

Read Matthew 13:1-8, 18-23

B lack people have no history, no heroes, no great moments."
This comment by his fifth-grade teacher motivated Arthur
Alfonso Schomburg (1874–1938) to devote his lifetime to
providing the world with an understanding of people of African
descent. Schomburg, born in Puerto Rico, moved to New York in
1891. He traveled internationally and collected letters, manuscripts,
among other items by persons of African descent. By 1926 he had
collected thousands of items. The Carnegie Corporation purchased
these items and placed them in the New York Public Library. Known
today as The Schomburg Center for Research in Black Culture, the
center houses more than five million items. Schomburg's focus on
providing understanding is a legacy for the world.

The parable of the sower also focuses on understanding. This
story shows that we can live fruitful lives when we hear and understand the word of God. Just as Arthur Schomburg devoted himself
to extensive study and research concerning Black culture, we too
must devote study to the Scriptures to be deeply rooted in our faith.
We do not want to be like a path, rocky or thorny place, where the
word can be easily uprooted. Instead we want to be the good soil.

Are you good soil? Are you receiving the word with understanding?

Prayer: Dear God, I want to receive your word with understanding so
that I will be productive in your kingdom.

**Woodson published The Education of the Negro Prior to 1861
(1915).**

THURSDAY, FEBRUARY 10, 2005

THE MUSTARD SEED

Do not despise these small beginnings.
(Zechariah 4:10*a*, NLT)

Read Matthew 13:31-32

I am a woman that came from the cotton fields of the South. I was promoted from there to the wash-tub. Then I was promoted to the cook kitchen, and from there I promoted myself into the business of manufacturing hair goods and preparations."

And the rest is history for Sarah Breedlove, known as Madam C. J. Walker (1867–1919). Walker, the first African American woman millionaire, is credited with inventing the straightening comb. She, like many successful African Americans, has a story of humble beginnings. Walker stated, "I am not ashamed of my past. I am not ashamed of my humble beginning."

The parable of the mustard seed is one of small beginnings, from a tiny seed to a tree providing shade and shelter. The gospel, like the mustard seed, had a humble beginning—the Savior of the world was born in a barn. But now the gospel is being preached worldwide.

Too often we discount small beginnings. We are always looking for the biggest, the greatest, and the latest. But God doesn't discount smallness. He knows what is best for us. He is the Alpha and Omega, and knows our end: "I am God, and there is no one like me, declaring the end from the beginning. . . . My purpose shall stand, and I will fulfill my intention" (Isaiah 46:9*a*-10).

Prayer: O Creator, who has ordained my end, help me to be appreciative of all things—especially small things.

Woodson published A Century of Negro Migration (1918).

A'Lelia Bundles, *On Her Own Ground: The Life and Times of Madam C.J. Walker* (New York: Scribner, 2001).

FRUITFULLY SPEAKING

The tree is known by its fruit.
(Matthew 12:33*b*)

Read Matthew 12:33-37

Fruit testifies. Like a true witness it reveals who we are. Jesus' analogy of a tree and its fruit admonishes us to be mindful of what we think, say, and do. Whatever is in our heart is what we will produce. If we are evil, then what we produce will be evil. This evil fruit has a negative effect on others and us. And it may appear as jealousy, strife, unforgiveness, and hatred. If we are good, what we produce, our fruit, will be good. We are always producing something; and if we are connected to the True Vine, our fruit will bless God and others. This fruit might appear as joy, peace, longsuffering, and hope. Fruit testifies.

Charles Albert Tindley's (1851–1933) fruit testified in song. Tindley, who was a renowned pastor and hymn writer, produced nearly fifty hymns. Among his well-known songs are "We'll Understand It Better By and By," "Leave It There," and "I'll Overcome Someday" (a song from which the civil rights anthem "We Shall Overcome" derived). One of his songs, "Nothing Between," speaks of renouncing sinful pleasure. Tindley did not want anything to come between him and his Savior.

Our fruit will testify too if we let nothing hinder our relationship with God. We can let it speak of God's salvation, goodness, and mercy through our lifestyle. Go testify!

Prayer: O True Vine, search my heart and reveal any areas in my life that are producing spoiled fruit. Help me to abide in you and produce a harvest pleasing in your sight.

Woodson was the principal at Armstrong Manuel Training School, Washington, D.C. (1918–1919).

BARREN FIG TREE

Cut it down! Why should it be wasting the soil?
(Luke 13:7*b*)

Read Luke 13:6-9

The fig tree was not fulfilling its purpose. It was taking up space, living off the nutrients of the soil but producing nothing. The owner was ready to cut it down. For three years it had produced nothing, and in the eyes of the owner it had wasted the soil.

If we liken the fig tree owner to God, and we as Christians fig trees, then we can gather from this parable that God expects us to be fruitful and productive for his kingdom. There's no time for wasting the soil.

One scientist and educator used the soil to its fullest capacity. George Washington Carver (1864?–1943) performed pioneering research in agriculture and plant chemistry. He developed more than 300 products from the peanut, more than 100 products from the sweet potato, 75 products from the pecan, and over 500 dyes and pigments from 28 different plants. Some of these products include rubbing oils, shaving cream, wood stains, ink, shampoo, and meat tenderizer. But that's not all. Carver conceived the idea of crop rotation as a means of restoring soil and developed a new method of organic fertilization. Carver did not waste the soil.

Carver was not only a brilliant scientist, he was also a devout Christian. He once stated, "I work together with God. God has shown me the secrets of the peanut." As we work with God, being submissive to his will, we too will be productive for the kingdom.

Prayer: Lord, I don't want to waste your soil.

Woodson: "Ancient Africans . . . knew sufficient science to concoct poisons for arrowheads, to mix durable colors for paintings, to extract metals from nature and refine them for development in the industrial arts."
(The Mis-Education of The Negro).

CONSIDER THE COST

He started something he couldn't finish.
(Luke 13:30)

Read Luke 14:25-30

What does it take to be a disciple? Jesus knew the crowd that followed him did not truly understand what it meant. So he tells this story about a builder. He concludes the story by stating that if the builder is unable to finish then everyone will say, "He started something he couldn't finish."

One word sums up Jesus' parable: *commitment.* Jesus wanted his listeners to understand that following him would require commitment. Not partial commitment—"Jesus I will follow you until"—but a dedication that says "I will follow you all the way."

Harriet Tubman (circa 1820–1913), the great conductor of the Underground Railroad and a God-fearing woman, herald the value of going all the way. Helping people escape slavery was extremely dangerous, so Tubman could not afford to have half-committed followers. She was known to force double-minded slaves to freedom by pointing a gun at them and saying "You'll be free or die." As a result she never used her gun, led more than three hundred slaves to freedom, and never lost one.

Christ Jesus also offers us freedom from bondage, the bondage of sin and death (John 3:86; Romans 8:2). What will it require to gain and maintain this freedom? We must be disciples willing to give up our ways of doing things and follow him with all our heart (Luke 14:33). Our story does not have to end with "He started something he couldn't finish," because our God is gracious and provides strength to help us as we serve him (Philippians 1:6). So as we consider the cost of following Jesus, we can rest assured that he will never leave nor forsake us.

Prayer: Jesus, I am your disciple. I will follow you all the way.

**Woodson was Dean of the School of Liberal Arts,
Howard University (1919–1920).**

HIDDEN TREASURE

We have this treasure in earthen vessels,
that the excellence of the power may be of God and not of us.
(2 Corinthians 4:7, NKJV)

Read Matthew 13:44-45

Valuables are protected. They are placed in vaults, behind glass cases, under lock and key, and often out of sight. The man in this story discovered a valuable. He placed it in the ground, which was considered the bank or secure place during biblical times. But hiding this treasure was not sufficient. Further securing was needed. So the man, estatic over his find, sold all that he had and bought the field where he buried the treasure. It was thus secured.

As Christians we, like the man in this story, have a treasure. And our treasure too is in the earth, or rather in us who are earthen vessels. The treasure is salvation through Jesus Christ. When we consider all Christ offers, we are compelled to give up all we have in service to him. Paul says, "Nothing is as wonderful as knowing Christ Jesus my Lord. I have given up everything else" (Philippians 3:8, CEV).

Giving up all for Christ is a daily goal. We must hide this treasure, the word of God, in our hearts. This will enable us to be firmly grounded (Psalm 119:11). As we hide the word in our heart, God hides us in his mercy and love. Our life becomes hidden with Christ (Colossians 3:3). This does not mean that we keep the word to ourselves. Quite the contrary. We share salvation with others through the living out of a godly life.

African American history has been full of hidden treasures—treasures of a great heritage. We can be grateful for historians like Woodson and others who unearthed the riches of our culture through their commitment to education.

Prayer: Lord, you are my treasure. Nothing is more valuable than you.

Woodson organized Associated Publishers (1920).

UNFORGIVING CONFINES

Bear with one another and forgive whatever grievance
you may have against one another. Forgive as the Lord forgave you.
(Colossians 3:13)

Read Matthew 18:22-25

A servant owed the king millions of dollars, but did not have the money to repay. Can you imagine the servant's reaction when the king showed mercy and exonerated the servant's debt? That servant, however, did not show someone who owed him money the same courtesy. Although the servant's debtor owed only a few dollars, he refused to forgive the man. Instead the servant demanded payment and imprisoned his debtor.

When we do not forgive, we place our own lives in prison. We are in the cell of bitterness, with our heart handcuffed to hate.

Is forgiveness easy? No. While God does not want us to be doormats, welcoming unjust acts, he does require us to forgive our offenders. And Jesus says we must forgive seventy times seven. This does not denote a limited forgiveness, but rather limitless forgiveness.

Rubin Carter (1937–), a prize boxer, spent nearly twenty years in prison for a crime he did not commit. He was cleared of all charges in 1985. In the movie *The Hurricane,* based on his life, Carter (portrayed by Denzel Washington) makes a powerful statement: "Hate put me in prison; love is going to bust me out."

So each time we decide not to forgive we must think about Christ who freely forgives us. This is what the king wanted the forgiven servant to keep in mind. When the king heard that the servant did not forgive his debtor, the king was outraged and had the ungrateful man thrown in prison. This man's imprisonment was due to his own unforgiveness. Being unforgiving imprisons others and us. But the love of God can "bust us out."

Prayer: Lord, keep me out of the prison of unforgivingness.

Woodson received a grant from Carnegie Institution (1921).

DEEP IN DEBT

The one to whom little is forgiven, loves little.
(Luke 7:47*b*)

Read Luke 7:41-47

A sinful woman, a prostitute, enters Simon the Pharisee's house and does something shocking. She anoints Jesus' feet with perfume. Discerning Simon's puzzled mind, Jesus uses this woman's action as the basis for a parable. This is the story: Two people were in debt. One owed a banker 50 silver coins while another owed 500 silver coins. Neither had the money to pay the debt. Once again, as in the story in Matthew 18:22-25, the creditor shows mercy and cancels the debt. While both debtors are grateful for the mercy shown them, the one who had the 500 coins canceled will no doubt have greater appreciation.

All of us are indebted to Christ, who so graciously paid the penalty of our sins. Our debt is the obligation to live a life of godliness (Romans 8:12; Galatians 5:3). Although each of us has had varying experiences, all of us need God's forgiveness. Marjorie Kimbrough says that the woman was so filled with gratitude that she took the role of a host, Simon's role: "The servant role and hospitality with which she had greeted the Lord were those that a more loving host would have shown. But because Simon was a Pharisee, an interpreter of the Law, he probably felt himself guilty of little or no sin for which to be forgiven. Therefore, he had little or no love to extend."

Let's always remember God deserves all our love, our whole-hearted devotion. Each day God provides us with new mercies that should cause us to offer thanks.

Prayer: Gracious Redeemer, thank you for canceling my debt.

Woodson published The Negro in Our History *(1922).*

Marjorie L. Kimbrough, *She Is Worthy: Encounters with Biblical Women* (Nashville: Abingdon Press, 1994).

THURSDAY, FEBRUARY 17, 2005

DON'T STOP KNOCKING

Don't bother me! The door is bolted. . . .
I cannot get up to give you something.
(Luke 11:7, CEV)

Read Luke 11:5-8

Knock. *knock, knock, knock. Knock, knock, knock, knock, knock. Knock, knock, knock, knock, knock! Knock, knock, knock, knock, knock, knock, knock, knock, knock!!! Knock, knock, knock,knock!!!!* The knocks on the friend's door only grew longer and louder.

To get peace and provide rest for his family, the friend answered the door and gave the visitor what he wanted: three loaves of bread.

Jesus tells the disciples this story of persistence when one of his disciples requests, "Lord, teach us to pray." Jesus knows how weary and double-minded we can become when it seems as if our prayers are unanswered. He doesn't want us to give up, but to hold on to our faith and keep on praying.

One determined young woman kept the faith that she would enter law school. Joylyn Wright knocked consistently on the admissions doors of numerous law schools. After many rejections, she realized she needed to rely on God. Her testimony is "Persistence Overrides Resistance": "Having received thirty-seven rejection letters, countless negative advice and an academic suspension in college . . . this kid from a single-parent home in rural South Carolina was finally accepted to law school."

So don't stop praying. God is listening. Just as the man knocked with persistence, his persistence was filled with hope and expectation. God wants us to be filled with the same.

Prayer: Lord, help me to knock with persistence.

Woodson established Negro History Week (1926), which became Black History Month in 1976.

Joylyn Wright in Travis Smiley, *Keeping the Faith* (New York: Doubleday, 2002).

GOD'S EEOC

These last worked . . . one hour, and you have made them equal to us.
(Matthew 20:16)

Read Matthew 20:1-16

Thurgood Marshall (1908–1993), the first African American Supreme Court justice, was a fearless defender of civil rights. Known as Mr. Civil Rights, Marshall overturned many separate-but-equal laws and won the case against school segregation in 1954. This landmark case was known as *Brown v. Board of Education*. He once stated, "My commitments have always been to justice for all people, regardless of race, creed, or color." He was a fighter for equality.

Equality is the main issue that today's parable presents. The first group of workers think the landowner miscalculates by paying all workers the same amount. So they complain. But the workers make an agreement for a certain amount, and the landowner pays them as promised.

God is the landowner. His definition of equality is not the same as ours. God does not look at our collars—whether white, blue, or polka-dotted—when he employs us for kingdom work. He is an Equal Opportunity Employer. A person who accepts God's call to work, then becomes pastor of a megachurch, labors 50 years, leads thousands to Christ, and dies will go to heaven. Or if a notorious criminal who has committed acts of violence for 50 years repents and accepts God's call to work one day, then dies the next, he too will go to heaven. You see, God is founder of the EEOC (Equal Employment Opportunity Commission). In his human resources office hangs a sign that says, "Whosoever will . . . "

Prayer: Lord, thank you for being a God of justice who invites everyone, regardless of race, creed, or color, to work in your kingdom.

Woodson: "We should emphasize not Negro History, but the Negro in history. What we need is not a history of selected races or nations, but the history of the world, void of national bias, race, hate, and religious prejudice."

TWO SONS AND A VINEYARD

"I go, sir"; but he did not.
(Matthew 21:30*b*)

Read Matthew 21:28-32

Too often we make promises and agreements but do not keep them. It sounds and looks good to say, "Sure, I can do that"; "Oh, I will be there"; "Yes, you can count on me." This is what the second son did. He looked good in front of his father when he said, "I go, sir. " And perhaps he even glared condescendingly upon his brother, who had the audacity to say no.

Jesus directs this parable to the Pharisees, who represent the second son. These religious leaders maintain the appearance of saying yes to God or "I go, sir" by doing righteous deeds such as fasting, tithing, ritual cleansings. But in their hearts and by the fruit that their lives produce they are actually saying, "I will not go work in your vineyard." Jesus says the Pharisees uphold the law by performing pious acts but omit important matters such as justice, mercy, and faith (Matthew 23:23).

The first son, on the other hand, has a change of heart and goes to work in the vineyard. This son realizes the error of his ways and repents. This son does the will of the Father. The second son not only does not repent but also does not feel the need to do so.

Repentance, then, is the focus of this story. When we respond with a heart of submission, then we do the Father's will.

Prayer: Father, help me to do your will today.

Woodson received the Spingarn Medal in 1926. (Instituted in 1914, the NAACP awards this medal yearly to an outstanding African American.)

"STANDIN' IN THE NEED OF PRAYER"

The Pharisee, standing by himself, was praying thus. . . .
The tax collector, standing far off, would not even look up to heaven.
(Luke 18:11, 13)

Read Luke 18:9-14

Two men stood in the temple—standing in the need of prayer. One was a Pharisee, the other a tax collector. Using the words of the Negro spiritual "Standin' in the Need of Prayer," the Pharisee would sound like this: "It's those robbers, evildoers, and tax collectors, O Lord / Standin' in the need of prayer." The tax collector, however, would sound like this: "Not the Pharisee or others, but it's me, O Lord / Standin' in the need of prayer."

We can learn much from these two prayers. The Pharisee's prayer was filled with pride, the tax collector's with humility. The Pharisee's prayer was judgmental. Even his position of "standing by himself" confirms his prideful attitude. The tax collector was penitent. He felt so unworthy to address God that he stood far off and didn't look up. Theologian and educator Howard Thurman (1900–1981) stated that we judge ourselves when we judge others: "It is very easy to sit in judgment upon the behavior of others but often difficult to realize that every judgment is a self-judgment."

Where are you standing when you pray? Is it in the judgment position of the Pharisee or in the humble position of the tax collector?

Prayer: Lord, I do not want to look down on others. Please give me a humble spirit.

Woodson published Negro Makers of History *(1928).*

SITTIN' IN THE NEED OF PRAYER

For all who exalt themselves will be humbled,
and those who humble themselves will be exalted.
(Luke 14:11)

Read Luke 14:7-11

The Pharisees had a problem with position. It really did not matter what position the Pharisees took—standing, sitting, kneeling— they were in need of prayer. Since prayer is communing with God, they were in need of a genuine relationship with God. In this parable the physical place where they sat—in the higher seat—was an indication of where they sat spiritually. The seat of pride.

Yet God calls us to be humble. Humility allows us to see the truth about ourselves. Pride has a way of making us think we have position or status that we do not have. Dr. Samuel Proctor (1921–1997) says pride deceives: "If you don't pause and worship God in the beauty of holiness, you will always call things by the wrong names and think you've told the truth."

Let's choose our seats carefully. Let's not sit up high in the seat of pride. God demotes those who take this seat. Rather, let's sit in humility. No, let's recline in humility, providing God the opportunity to exalt us.

Prayer: Lord, help me to give up my position filled with pride and to take a humble seat.

Woodson published The Mis-Education of The Negro *(1933)*.

SALT

You are the salt of the earth.
(Matthew 5:13*a*)

Read Matthew 5:13

Salt functions as a preservative. It holds back corruption and adds flavor. These two functions should be a part of our nature as Christians.

Leontine Turpeau Current Kelly, the first African American woman elected bishop in a mainline denomination, is salt in the United Methodist Church. In *Breaking Barriers,* her daughter Angella Current explains that she was a powerful voice for change within the denomination:

> Bishop Kelly used her voice and personality to influence the Council of Bishops as they debated the moral issues of the day and the church's role and responsibilities. Being in the midst of more than one hundred active and retired bishops at the biannual Council of Bishops meetings, the majority of them being white males over fifty-five years of age, did not appear to intimidate her . . . with a strong prophetic voice, she never failed to get their attention.

Bishop Kelly has received numerous awards and more than ten honorary doctorate degrees. In her role as bishop, Kelly stated, "I will not model a leadership role that will not be caring and understanding."

We are called to be salt for the kingdom of God. May our actions and words be filled with salt: "Let your speech always be gracious, seasoned with salt, so that you may know how you ought to answer everyone" (Colossians 4:6). Are you adding godly flavor in your community church, job, and spheres of influence?

Prayer: Lord, help me to add a godly flavor to all the places you might send me.

Woodson began publishing the Negro History Bulletin *in 1937*.

Angella Current, *Breaking Barriers: An African American Family & the Methodist Story* (Nashville: Abingdon Press, 2001).

WEDNESDAY, FEBRUARY 23, 2005

LET YOUR LIGHT SHINE

*Let your light shine before others, so that they may
see your good works and give glory to your Father in heaven.*
(Matthew 5:15)

Read Luke11:33-36; Matthew 5:13-16

Power failures are a vivid reminder of how we often take light
for granted. We cease immediate activities, grope in darkness,
and guide ourselves through dimmed corridors. We light can-
dles, beam flashlights, and use whatever light available. When the
power is restored, we are grateful.

As Christians we are an important light source, so important that
Jesus calls us "the light of the entire world." What an immense
responsibility, a phenomenal privilege, a spiritual service. How can
we provide light? It is only through Jesus. As we develop an intimate
relationship with God, we are able to reflect the light of Christ.

Our ancestors knew this truth as they proclaimed, "This little
light of mine, I'm going to let it shine." William B. McClain says,
"Even though their lives seemed to be surrounded by shadows and
darkness, their faith assured them that they were 'the light of the
world.'"

Our faith can assure us too that we bring light where we live. As
we strive to live a life that pleases God, then others will see our light,
our good deeds, and glorify God.

Prayer: Lord, today I choose to let your light reflect through me.

**Woodson: *"Let the light of history enable us to see that enough of good
there is in the lowest estate to sweeten life, enough of evil in the highest to
check presumption; enough there is of both in all estates to bend us in
compassionate brotherhood."***

William McClain, *Come Sunday: The Liturgy of Zion* (Nashville: Abingdon Press, 1990).

THURSDAY, FEBRUARY 24, 2005

DO YOU SEE WHAT I MEAN?

*A Samaritan while traveling came near him;
and when he saw him, he was moved with pity.*
(Luke 10:33)

Read Luke10:30-37

Do you see what I mean? We ask this to confirm that our listener understands us. Jesus asks the same question when he tells a parable, wanting his listeners to understand and see with spiritual eyes.

This parable on being a good neighbor is all about seeing. The priest and the Levite see a half-dead man on the Jericho road. But they see more. They see a man who could potentially defile them. According to Numbers 19:11, it was against the Jewish law to touch a dead person. Obeying the law is more important than taking a risk to help this man, so the priest and Levite cross to the other side.

The Samaritan sees a half-dead man on the Jericho road. But he sees more. He sees a person who has fallen, is brutally beaten, and is abandoned. The Samaritan sees with eyes filled with compassion. He could not cross over to the other side but draws near.

This is a story of God's compassion. It is a story of a Samaritan, a race the Jews despised, who shows unconditional love. The Samaritan sees a fellow human being in need and declares him a neighbor. He gives. He gives of his time, of himself, and of his resources. Maya Angelou (1928–) says, "The New Testament informs the reader that it is more blessed to give than to receive. I have found that among its other benefits, giving liberates the soul of the giver." The Samaritan is liberated. He is not bound by prejudices. He sees. *Do you see what I mean?*

Prayer: O Omniscient God, please give me spiritual eyes.

Woodson received Doctor of Laws from West Virginia State College (1941).

Maya Angelou, *Wouldn't Take Nothing for My Journey Now* (New York: Random House, 1993).

A LOVER OF THE LOST

There is rejoicing in the presence of the
angels of God over one sinner who repents.

Read Luke 15:1-10

God's love is incomprehensible. We sing about God's love, preach and teach on his love, but we still cannot understand it. God loves us, and that's fact. We know God loves us not merely by what he says, but by what he does.

The parables on the lost sheep, the lost coin, and the lost son all demonstrate the love of God. One characteristic of God's love is his devotion to the lost. Jesus says plainly, "For the Son of Man came to seek and to save what was lost" (Luke 19:10, NIV). The Pharisees never grasp the love that Jesus shows to the lost. It is this lack of understanding that prompts Jesus to tell the parables of lostness. While the tax collectors attend to Jesus' words, the Pharisees murmur: "This man welcomes sinners and eats with them" (Luke 15:1, NIV). The Pharisees' narrow-mindedness could not comprehend a love that embraces sinners. Jesus' love is so wide that it encompasses all states of lostness. As William Barclay noted, it does not matter if one is lost because of carelessness (the sheep), or lost due to no fault of its own (the coin), or lost deliberately (the son). In fact the son who squanders his inheritance never gives his repentance speech. When the son returns, his father sees him at a distance and welcomes the son with a party. What love! African Bishop Augustine of Hippo (A.D., 354–430) stated, "There is no greater invitation to love than loving first."

God loved us first. Now we should love God and others.

Prayer: Gracious God, thank you for your steadfast, incomprehensible love.

Woodson was elected to the Ebony Hall of Fame (1958).

TALENTS WITH VISION

I was afraid and I went and hid your talent in the ground.
(Matthew 25:25)

Read Matthew 25:14-30

Well done, good and faithful servant! Each of us desires to hear God say these words to us. Two of the servants in this parable heard these gracious words concerning the talents given them. A talent, which was actually a weight, was worth a thousand dollars or more. The servants with five and two talents do not waste them, but in fact double their value. These servants have a vision, act on their vision, and are thus productive. But the servant with the one talent does not have a plan for his money. Instead he hides it in the ground. This person without vision and action hears words of rebuke from the owner.

We need a God-given vision to accompany our gifts and talents, so that God can accomplish in us what he wills. Mary McLeod Bethune (1875–1955) had a vision for black women in America. In 1904 she founded the Daytona Normal and Industrial Institute for Negro Girls (now Bethune-Cookman College). Her vision was to see young women educated: "I am blessed with the power to visualize and to see a mental picture of what I would desire. I am always building spiritual air castles. Only those with a spiritual understanding can appreciate my feelings when I say I saw in my mind's eye the Bethune-Cookman College of today."

We too must not bury our talents, but move forward with our visions and fulfill God's purpose. As we become good stewards of our gifts and talents, we invest not only in our own lives but also the lives of others.

Prayer: God, help me to be productive—not wasting anything—with the gifts you have given to me.

Woodson: "Real education means to inspire people to live more abundantly, to learn to begin with life as they find it and make it better."
(The Mis-Education of The Negro).

IN GOD'S CARE

I tell you, do not worry about your life.
(Matthew 6:31a, NIV)

Read Matthew 6:25-34; 10:29

In an age of moral decay and war, it is sometimes difficult not to worry. We worry about our children, our families, our safety, our money. These concerns consume us, and we are filled with anxiety. The Scriptures tell us to trust God, but sometimes we feel God is not moving fast enough to address our immediate need.

Then Jesus directs us to examine how he holds creation in his care. First, the birds do not plant gardens, but God takes care of them. Next, God adorns the short-lived lilies with beauty. *That is wonderful for birds and lilies,* we might think, *they don't have to pay bills, put children through college, or work in a stressful environment.* Yet that's the point that Jesus makes in this parable. He takes care of birds and flowers; though valuable, they are not as valuable as we are in the sight of God. So if he provides beauty and food for the least of his creation, he will take care of us. He sees and knows our every step.

God sees all our concerns too. We are valuable to him. So as we encounter daily concerns, just remember our Almighty Father has us in his care. Frances Harper (1825–1911), writer and abolitionist, spoke of God's omniscient care for a fallen bird in her poem "The Sparrow." She sums up God's love for us well in this stanza of her poem:

Oh, restless heart, learn thou to trust
In God, so tender, strong and just
In whose love and mercy everywhere
His humblest children have a share.

Prayer: Dear God, thank you that I'm safe in your care.

Woodson published numerous articles throughout his lifetime.

Emma J. Wisdom, *Poems by Frances Ellen Watkins Harper* (Nashville: Post Oak Publications, 1998). Used by permission.

I WANT TO BE READY

You must be ready all the time, for the
Son of Man will come when least expected. "
(Luke 12:40, NLT)

Read Luke 12:35-48

Down through the ages there have been many attempts to predict Christ's return. Edgar Whisenant predicted that Christ would return in 1988. Thousands of people believed him. But the Negro spiritual "I Want to Be Ready" has the right idea. A life of readiness is this parable's exhortation. Technology, which has tremendous capacity to make approximate weather predictions, cannot properly tell us when Christ will return. No one knows. So we must be ready. And we can be prepared. God is able to provide us victory, strength, and grace to enable us to stand ready.

In the end we have to live as though Christ could come any day—no, any minute. Delores Carpenter sums it well when she says we may not feel the imminence of Christ's return since it has been 2,000 years, but we still need to be watching: "Maybe Jesus hasn't come back, but you've got to live every day as though he's coming today. . . . We must live our lives on tiptoed expectancy that he is coming any minute. We still need to be alert and watching for the kingdom. This gives us hope and inspires us to do what the Lord has called us to do. . . . Every day may be the last minute. This may be my last time. I don't know."

Prayer: Lord, too often I become so consumed with the issues and concerns of my daily life that I forget you promised to return. Help me to live as though you are coming back today.

Woodson died April 5, 1950, in Washington, D.C.

Delores Carpenter, "Prophecy in Times Like These" in *9.11.01: African American Leaders Respond to an American Tragedy* (Valley Forge, Penn.: Judson Press, 2001).